Think With Me

Tasmin Lowe

Book Cover by Katia Nunes

Edited by Astri Saestad

Print ISBN: 978-0-6397-8451-9
E-book ISBN: 978-0-6397-8452-6

First edition 2023

Contents

Who is *Me?*

Eunoia

Beautiful thinking, a well mind.

Consider this a preface or introduction that casually turns into a baby chapter. A way to introduce myself, my book, and my very important disclaimer that this is purely written from my own perspective, thoughts, and experiences, and not a complicated scientifically researched work. Rather, a personal, emotional and vulnerable introspection before reeling you in with some introvert 101 discussions. It's interesting though, I promise.

Think With Me invites you to take a closer look inside an introverted mind – specifically mine – so that you can relate, better understand, or just have something to read to help you fall asleep.

In order to 'think with me', you need to know who I am. Let us start with the basics, shall we?

My name is Tasmin Lowe (formerly Copley), I am twenty-five years old as I begin to write this and my quarter-of-a-century self and experiences will be preserved within the pages of this book. I married my incredible husband, Andrew, in 2018 and we have a Pitbull fur baby, Koda. I'm a practicing Catholic, eat almost everything, love all things Disney, am a Harry Potter fanatic, adore wildlife and nature, enjoy (and occasionally fall asleep to) true crime content, and love to be creative. If it feels like I've invited you to class for a show-and-tell, I apologise. Perhaps you can tell this is my first book. Full disclosure, I would never actually invite anyone to a show-and-tell because of my performance anxiety and innate fear of being the centre of attention.

You may be thinking that at twenty-five there cannot be too much to tell, but I hope to surprise you. My writing style is essentially my thoughts and speech patterns slapped onto paper. See, I am not entirely capable of having this conversation aloud with many (if any) human beings, but if I were, this is what I would sound like and how I would tell it. As terrified as I am to put myself out there in this way, I am grateful for the talent to write and the opportunity to attempt – emphasis on attempt – to translate a mind like mine. You can count yourself lucky to have this raw, rare and real encounter of an introverted mind, it's not a common occurrence.

I have a degree in Communications which, as you read my book, you may find somewhat ironic. I studied via correspondence (naturally) with The University of South Africa and kept any necessary interactions online. Coincidentally, the conversation around why I never imagined myself attending a brick-and-mortar university sparked my inspiration to write this book in the first place. After being asked (again), I thought to myself (again) 'I've answered questions like this enough times, maybe I should just write a book fully explaining myself.' And well, here I am. For those who are still wondering, the answer is: thinking about navigating a university campus, meeting whole classes of new people, and first-year shenanigans just freaked me out.

Over the past few years, I have worked in different facets of the marketing industry in various roles, none of which I would consider my dream job. Right now, I am still unsure as to what I want to do 'forever' or even 'for now', but this book, I feel, is a step in the *write* direction (get it?). The topic of my career has always been a touchy one for me. I have at least one breakdown about it every year. I haven't had lightbulb moments of clarity regarding my professional future or what it is I want to do with my life. Trust me, it's frustrating.

Most people would look to their childhood dreams for career inspiration – as a child I wanted to own the Kruger National Park... mostly because I wanted all the wild animals to be my real-life teddies. In my next phase of life, the idea was to drop out of high school in grade 10 and go into coaching gymnastics full-time, which, at the time, I had only been doing for a year. Considering that the gymnastics club I was part of only operated after school hours anyway, it made sense for me to suck it up and finish school, besides, I wasn't going to be 'that kid.' Also, my parents wouldn't allow it – essentially, I had no choice and retrospectively it wasn't that bad. After high school and a productive gap year at a performing arts college, it became a matter of looking to what I enjoyed most as inspiration for a pending career. This led to my Communications degree, which is about as general as they come - and so my journey to purpose continued at a plateaued rate.

I know there are many things I can do and enjoy – photography, dancing, singing and, of course, writing – but I do not consider myself 'great' or 'exceptional' in those departments. I do, however, consider exceptionality a prerequisite to monetise or build a career out of a hobby or skill, which is problematic when one is their own greatest critic, such as myself. I have always loved writing and my creativity, but it never occurred to me to write a book because I could never think of a fictional story to create. The poetry I have written is, in my opinion, sub-par for publishing and more for fun than anything else. Naturally, I did not and still don't quite, consider myself a viable topic for a book in any form. I have not done anything spectacular in my life, I am not an expert in any field, nor do I have any incredibly outrageous adventures to boast about. But what I do have, and what I have come to realise is quite unique, is my introverted mind and the way it works.

Everyone knows an introvert, but not everyone, introverts included, understand how their minds work or why their minds work the way they do. Now, although I am not academically qualified to talk about the scientific or psychological 'why', I would like to share with you a bit about the 'how', from my personal experiences.

A quick Google search defines an introvert as a shy, quiet person or someone who is predominantly concerned with their own thoughts and feelings rather than external concerns. Additionally, experience allows me to tell you that introverts are those typically drained by socialising, whereas extroverts are energized by it. As an introvert, I do define myself as someone who, yes, is shy, quiet, drained by social interactions and who spends most of my time conversing in my mind, but definitely not as someone who is not focussed on 'external concerns'. In fact, most of the reasons for why I shut down socially and what I internally obsess about has to do with what is happening around me. I could be standing in line at a store, walking into a shopping centre, accidentally lock eyes with a passing stranger, or be sitting in the silence of my own home and have multiple thoughts roaming around in my mind, reflecting through my behaviour.

Most people are under the impression that introverts don't have much to say, but this is a misconception. If people could spend a day inside my head, they would be surprised (and possibly highly concerned) to find that I actually have hundreds of conversations. Granted, they occur in my thoughts and are usually a variety of parallels of one conversation I've either already had with someone, or that which I imagine would happen if I were to send a train of thought from my mind, through to my lips and out in the open. Basically, I am the type of person who lives very much inside of their own mind – quiet on the outside, noisy and chaotic on the inside – as may be the case for most introverts.

There is a secret power in choosing to be quiet amongst the commotion of conversation - I say choosing but sometimes it's more of a surrendering, rather, to your inner anxiety. That power is the ability to listen and read between the lines, and when you live out every possible version of an event in your mind (daily), it's something that comes naturally. I go into more detail about this in chapter three, this is just to open your mind towards who introverts can be.

It's also important to note that there are different types of introverts. You might think this is pretty obvious as every individual has their own personality traits, quirks, values, talents and circumstances unique to themselves, but some still need the reminder. These traits make each of us unique, but with a few similarities under the 'introvert' umbrella. There are four types of introversion that have been observed, identified, and studied by psychologist Jonathan Cheek: the social, thinking, anxious and restrained introvert. Notice I said 'and' instead of 'or' in the list between introversion types. It is common to find that an introvert falls within a spectrum of more than one, if not a bit of each, introvert type. Social introverts prefer solitude, or only socialising within a small group of close friends and family. Thinking introverts are introspective, living inside the world their mind creates. Anxious introverts experience anxiety in most social or even individual scenarios due to their self-consciousness. And the restrained introverts are the overthinkers with slow reaction times in terms of their physical and psychological movement.

I like to think of myself as an overachiever because I feel that I fit perfectly into all four categories of introversion. I definitely prefer alone time to social events, I have my own world operating in my mind that tags along wherever I go, I experience anxiety in a variety of environments, am extremely self-conscious, and I overthink *everything*, which drives my procrastination and steals any go-getter attitude I may strive for. Told you, overachiever right here.

In this book I speak strictly from my experiences as an introvert and how I have been forced to explain myself, or deal with the consequences of my introversion. So, when I use the universal 'we', interpret it loosely because not every introvert is like me, but some of them may be. Another obvious note is that individuals are uniquely complex. There are a variety of motivations behind a person's actions and reactions. So, again, this book is purely based on my own personality and perspective of introversion. Ultimately, what I'm trying to achieve by sharing *my* story is that introverts, and those who can relate, would feel seen and understood. And an added bonus would be to just entertain each reader who tags along for the ride.

Believe me when I say I have done many a personality test in my life - you know, to be sure I am who I am and do indeed feature somewhere on the Myers-Briggs Type Indicator scale. My results are always between these two categories depending on the day: INFP and INFJ. Introversion, Intuition, Feeling and Perception or Judging, respectively. A Mediator and Advocate.

Sounds about right. As someone who has grown up through her introversion; made life-long best friends by accident, been ruled by her emotions, and noticed every possible 'don't take it personally' (and taken it personally), I certainly see myself reflected in many aspects of these personality descriptions.

Personality tests can be helpful to gain a brief understanding of your general strengths, weaknesses, habits and how you operate in relationships. But the keyword here is *general.* You may read those summaries and relate to some, but not necessarily all the information provided. In writing this book, I hope to fill in some of the personality gaps fellow introverts may have yet to discover and understand about themselves through relatable and personal experiences. These are trade secrets, you know.

The purpose of *Think With Me* is to let you know that you are not alone and that it is not an impossible quest, or too great an ask to be understood. With my mind's words I hope this content encourages understanding and elaborates on introverted behaviour in a way that not many introverts have aptly expressed (despite deeply longing to).

Right, I think you have a good enough idea about who I am. Through my stories, you'll come to know me better than even my friends and family do.

My Personal Comforts

Numinous

To describe an overwhelming feeling of inspiration and spirituality in a personal experience. The powerful feeling of being overwhelmed and inspired.

Self-confidence is neither a familiar nor comfortable concept to me, so when I enter into anything, whether I know I am qualified or not, I do so hesitantly. Actually, the only place I carry confidence is on my nails. Stay with me here. My fingernails are such a small part of me, but are probably the most socially interactive - I use my hands to greet, exchange money for necessities, fix stray hairs, pet my dog, hold my husband's hand, comfort a friend, readjust my clothes, use my phone and, of course, type out this book. My hands are able to start a conversation when words would, otherwise, never escape my thoughts.

You can imagine how I feel right now, stuck at home during a national lockdown in a worldwide pandemic, with no access to my nail technician, while writing my first book about something as intimate as my mind. One of my personal comforts is my artistically designed, gel-manicured nails. It is something I rely on to make me feel good about and confident in myself. For an introvert with social and other anxieties, confidence in any form is quite welcome. More than how they look (which by my 'nail goals' Pinterest board means gorgeous for life), gel makes my nails feel indestructible. If I even just think about operating with bare, fragile nails my skin breaks out into goosebumps.

Socks are another comfort of mine. People who complain that all they get for Christmas and birthdays are socks are not my kind of people. Walking around in socks is as close as I get to walking around barefoot (cringe). If I have a trusty pair of socks on, I feel less stressed. It's as simple as that, but I will elaborate for those who are currently reading, losing interest and questioning their taste in books - I assure you that the rest of this book does not focus on hands and feet. My first gynaecologist appointment was scheduled after work, so I was wearing a pair of pumps – non-sock shoes. I specifically packed a pair of my favourite socks because I was so anxious about the appointment. I kid you not, I felt just that bit more comfortable once I had put on the inconvenient 'gown' and slipped my socks on... well as comfortable as one can be in that first-time situation.

I'm sure many of us have a go-to 'crutch' to help manage difficult or uncomfortable situations. I mean, something as insignificant as socks and superficial as pretty nails can provide me with a confidence boost and feeling of protection. Yes, I know socks won't stop my toes from being squashed, but I would do a lot more in a pair of socks than I would barefoot. There's a physical vulnerability I associate with being barefoot, which adds to my anxiety. Horror films depicting entities who tug people's feet while they're in bed have made it near impossible for me to sleep without socks on, even in the height of summer. By all means demon, grab my foot but please leave my socks on! I'll be that much braver because of it. The logic behind the protective comfort socks provide may not be sound, I can acknowledge that. Regardless, having that physical barrier between my skin and the unknown, however thin, is comforting.

My anxiety from interacting with unfamiliar things against my bare skin is caused by my tactile sensitivity. Be it something wet on the floor or floating in dishwater (gross). I am so aware of what I touch and how it makes my skin feel. If I run my finger over an unexpectedly cold surface, that touch, however instant, will stay with me for a good few hours and even affect the way I use my hands. With socks, gel-manicured nails and rubber gloves on, I feel as if I could touch or do almost anything. That thin layer of protection eases my anxiety and general discomforts.

Needless to say, I clearly have a mild form of obsessive-compulsive disorder. So much so that when I accidentally bump my left elbow on the door, I have to deliberately bump the right elbow

- in the exact place and with the same force - to even out the pain so that it doesn't feel like it 'stands out' on my skin. If I don't mimic to even the sensations out, it takes over my thoughts and makes me feel extremely uncomfortable and imbalanced. As you can imagine, new piercings and tattoos become slightly more challenging to manage in this regard. Not to mention that time I fractured my right ankle...

Physical vulnerability is where these comforts seem necessary to me. I would not be able to function like a (relatively) normal human being without them. As an introvert, I like to be in control of my situations and know exactly what is happening in and around me. I fear finding myself unprepared in an unknown or uncomfortable environment. I want to know that I am still in control even though I may have physically surrendered to my environment. Sounds impossible, but to counter this I have developed another personal comfort – a vivid imagination. When my eyes are closed, I don't stop seeing. Essentially, I never see 'black' behind my eyelids, but envision images that are as close a copy to my external environment as I can remember seeing, smelling, hearing or feeling in the moments before my eyes closed.

I refer to this as my tangible mind. Come with me to the spa for a massage and I'll describe this imagination-based comfort to you. First, know I've been low-key stressing since I made the appointment - trying to imagine a room I've never been inside of, a masseuse I've never met and the cover-up, towel-on-a-table, situation ahead of me (I'm convinced this will remain an awkward experience). Next, I do what I must to prepare: shave my legs, wear clothes that won't leave lines on my skin, paint my toes, and lug anti-perspirants and make-up around because heaven-forbid people realise I'm human. Now for the massage itself. I love a good massage and touch is my top love language. But, lying face down, half-naked, with my head in a hole and only a view of the floor is quite a vulnerable position. No socks allowed.

In these moments, where I have willingly forced myself to surrender to my environment, I turn to my trusty imagination. By this time I've had a good look at the room, been introduced to my masseuse and know which products will be used on my skin. When my eyes close in 'relaxation' (I am a rarely resting stress-ball), I start to recall everything around me as I had seen it and reimagine it as the experience changes. Call it a forced out-of-body experience where I follow the sounds and movement of the masseuse's hands as they massage my muscles and picture what that must look like; how my arm is lying after they readjust it, how to subtly shift it back into a comfortable position without offending them, the spot I missed while shaving that they're about to feel, hearing the hot stones and preparing my skin to feel them. This practice helps calm me down because it allows me to feel as if I still have some sort of grip on the situation... even if I mis-imagine everything, which is a great possibility.

My personal comforts provide a sense of control and physical protection against the vulnerabilities imposed by my environment. We aren't in a position to judge another's comforts, especially when we have our own. It's okay to be unsure about why someone performs certain rituals or uses specific items. But there is purpose behind what people do, even if they (the people or comforts) may seem a little strange (like myself). Respect doesn't always have to follow understanding and asking should precede assumptions. There is so much power, love and trust that comes from understanding one another, almost more so in simply *trying* and being *willing* to understand. Unfortunately, not all people think this way, which is why so many introverts and people who live with various mental health conditions feel targeted to the point where retreating seems to be their only option… for which they are further judged and accused of being anti-social, quiet, or otherwise.

There's almost always a rationale behind my introverted, quirky actions and reactions. Rather ask before calling me out on them otherwise I may lose the strength and comfort they bring me, placing me three steps back from where I've been fighting to progress to. Believe me, I'm very self-aware that I am the only one in the yoga class wearing socks, but I'm going to wear them anyway. If my downward dog slips into a plank, I'll just say it was planned – good for the core, right? In turn though, I need to learn to allow people to approach me in an attempt to genuinely try and understand me and not to take all forms of attention as an attack. Some of us like to take things personally. I know I need to work on that. There needs to be a balance of respect and willingness to understand each other that goes both ways in the communication line.

Quiet Communicators

Espirit d'escalier

The witty comeback you think of after the time has passed.

The mundanity of casual conversation between people, particularly as one of the participants, is a potentially stressful situation for an introvert. If I plan to meet a friend for coffee, I might do some preparation, much like I would for an upcoming job interview (an extremely stressful situation). There are certain factors that influence the necessity or degree of preparation required: the person I am meeting, when we last saw each other, how that encounter was (after a dozen replays in my mind), how often we communicate, and where we are going.

I make mental notes of questions to ask or topics to talk about just in case conversation grows quiet or the atmosphere feels awkward, which is likely since I will be there. I triple check the time and location as I don't want to end up at the wrong place, arrive too early and sit alone (which comes with the added stress of choosing where to sit), or arrive late and have them wait for me. Then I imagine how it will play out, starting with the hello hug and how not to be awkward about it – arriving early usually finds my foot stuck in the table legs, resulting in a clumsy, half-standing-half-stuck side(ish) hug.

All this mindful preparation usually happens en route so as not to psych myself out beforehand and bail instead. Sometimes, and this is very rare, I even practice my greetings, laughs, smiles, and faces in a mirror beforehand. Isn't it funny how the things we do (I do) to prevent public embarrassment are quite embarrassing anyway? I already know this will not be the first time I embarrass myself in this book, I say this as if I haven't done so already, so I'm just owning it.

Now, whether I have a conversation with a good friend, family member or acquaintance, the following remains true: I will hardly ever look you directly in the eye when I speak to you. But if I am being spoken to (and the conversation isn't awkward or super serious), I will happily engage in pupil-to-pupil contact. While I may not be looking into your eyes, I am likely reading your lips to decrease the chance of mishearing what you say. However, as soon as it's my turn to talk, my eyes will wander to the left, the skies, or a loose thread on my clothes. I might catch your eye, but not without blushing from the natural attention that comes with engaging in conversation. My vision is either blurry from overactive eyeballs or busy burning the pattern of the table's woodgrain into my mind, but I am still present and focused on our conversation.

Side note: because I do look at lips a lot, don't think I'm coming on to you or anything, it's just (somehow) less awkward for me than holding eye contact. I like to think it comes across friendlier than speaking to the empty airspace next you (which I sometimes do in extreme social anxiety inducing situations).

I promise I don't mean any offense when I do this, it's just extremely uncomfortable for me to look directly into someone's eyes - it's me, not you. In my mind, eye contact is an opportunity to watch a person judge me as I speak. It might sound silly, and I know the people in my life don't actively judge me, but it's one of those mind-consuming anxiety traits I associate with my introversion. The one person I can maintain the most eye contact with is my husband - I guess it helps that he has the most beautiful blue eyes on this planet - even then, if there is something especially difficult to say, I look away.

If I give advice, my opinion or just my pure honesty, I don't want to see it go in one ear and out the other. It's already difficult for me to hold a conversation, so when the moment to contribute does come, I don't want to physically see the disappointment, boredom, hurt or any negative acknowledgement of what I have to say - even if I know there is nothing that could be interpreted negatively from my words. For example, when I tell a joke or have a cheeky comeback – which I think is hilarious but is probably the equivalent of a 'dad joke' at best – I hesitate to vocalise even those thoughts. And you should know I really pride myself on my sense of humour and enjoy genuine laughter – be it mine or others'. Yes, I am an overthinker, but I am a quick (over)thinker with witty one-liner remarks and an inclination to think in puns. I know that not everything I say is as funny as I may think it is, or so I have been told, but I am not afraid to laugh at my own wit… or to instantly turn red and regret ever making my presence known. I never know with these things; sometimes it's easier to keep it to myself and refine the funny comment for a take-two attempt.

As an introvert with a small circle of cherished friends and family, I hold the people in my life in very high regard. I don't want to disappoint them in any way or even embarrass myself too much around them. I really just want them to continue liking me in the same capacity from which they grew to like to me and, sometimes, I feel I risk losing them whenever I open my mouth.

Your first few conversations with me might be more one-sided as it takes me a while to become comfortable enough to be completely myself around someone. I can still mimic an engaging conversation by appropriately reacting to what is said, ask questions to keep them talking and answer questions directed at me - I did learn a few tricks from my Communications degree after all, albeit predominantly the nonverbal aspects of communicating. Just know that I usually turn out to be a lot more than what my first impression offers.

On the contrary, if you were to have conversations with me via a digital device, you would meet the 'comfortable me' from the start. I may be slightly more polite initially, but I am not as afraid to be more myself through text than I am in person. Emoticons play a large role in this as I use them to cover my bad jokes and relay my inflections and intentions somewhat better than how my real-life facial expressions do.

In text, I also have more time to consider what I want to say and can edit my response until I'm happy with it, you know, instead of blurting out the first thing that comes to mind. See, if I take too long to respond in person, people may assume I am uninterested, which is hardly ever the case – a disassociated Tasmin has either already depleted her social battery or is in desperate need of a caffeine fix.

Text allows me to give my best advice without the stress of maintaining eye contact or witnessing negative responses to my words (blue ticks sting a little though). I can be tactfully honest through text messages and add a heart or flower emoji (relationship dependant) to remind the person it comes from a place of love. In this way, I am a quiet communicator - someone who has a lot to say but isn't always able to relay those messages appropriately in person. Unfortunately, my brain-to-mouth connection doesn't work as smoothly as my brain-to-keyboard connection. When I follow a conversation in person, I overthink bits of information I know I could contribute and by the time I muster the confidence to drop my refined golden nugget, something completely new is already being discussed.

Another face-to-face difficulty of mine is how much I am ruled and fuelled by my emotions, which can physically affect the way I speak and react. If I am angry, I shake, cry, lose my breath, and sometimes, laugh incredulously at anything said to me – it's just an uncomfortable experience for everyone involved. If I am proud, I remain on the verge of tears and my words catch in my throat. If I am confident, I automatically start to blush and am not always taken seriously after that, which usually leads to anger (we know how that goes). If I am passionate about something, the expression of love for it is usually relayed in a defensive-toned remark. If I am totally overwhelmed, consider me mentally checked out.

While I have somewhat (very slightly) mastered masking my emotions, at best it translates to shortened responses and tight-lipped smiles - all things easily set aside and filtered when chatting over text. Just enough for me to clearly communicate, support, or advise without emotional distraction.

As a quiet communicator, I require time to consider my responses before speaking because I need to ensure that how I respond leaves no room for miscommunication. Typing a response allows me to accurately word exactly what is going through my mind and proofread if necessary – it feels safe and effortless. The speed at which thoughts fill my mind is probably my fastest reflex. The speed at which they are processed and relayed as speech; significantly less so - especially with regards to new people and interactions.

Now, would you believe me if I told you that, given the choice, I would prefer one-on-one to group interaction? With much convincing though. I might be able to dodge speaking amongst a group, but there is still the possibility of a conversation starting around me, where *everyone* listens and awaits my reply. At that point, avoiding eye contact becomes more difficult and my potential for embarrassment greatly increases. In group gatherings, however, it is easier for me to step away from conversation and rather watch and listen to others in their interactions – introverts make great people-watchers.

This may sound like the typical 'introverts don't like people' storyline as I discuss my preferred type of human interaction, but I think that's another misconception about introverts – it's not that we don't like people or that we want to be isolated; rather that we like interacting within our own boundaries, a healthy sentiment for all people.

Earlier, I mentioned the secret power in choosing to be quiet amongst the commotion of conversation - this is where I elaborate. When you're a quiet introvert, you have more opportunities to really listen to what people say and observe the nonverbal cues that are usually overlooked. The struggle to maintain eye contact can be a strength in this way. I'm not justifying my, so called, 'bad manners' of looking away when I talk to you, I am simply pointing out the opportunity provided to observe the not-so-obvious signs regarding a person's true mental, emotional, or physical state.

Over the years I have become quite skilled at reading body language and dissecting people's reactions in correlation to what they say or how they respond. Okay, so not on a Cal Lightman, *Lie to Me,* detective level, but enough to help me be a better friend and socialite. When observing someone I know (and humans in general),

I quickly pick up on when they aren't quite themselves despite the front they put on. I pay enough attention to the verbal and nonverbal cues to recognize when someone is 'off'. I notice it in their messages, or lack thereof, based on their use of certain words and emojis. Like when my husband sends me a hug instead of a kiss emoji, I know he's just trying (and succeeding) to push my buttons. Also, I tend to visibly carry my emotions on my face and in my body language, so I know what it physically feels like and can imagine what it must look like to others (there's the out-of-body imaginative power of my mind again). Being this observant helps me communicate better because I can comment on or ask about what I notice, then process my deductions with the new information shared.

I actually enjoy conversations where I can sit back and listen to a person vent – without being labelled as quiet or shy – because it allows me to develop this skill and use it in a helpful manner. Thanks to my visual, hyperactive mind, I can picture and process everything they say - I imagine myself in their shoes. Basically, I'm the best person to talk to when you need a hype-woman to back you up by earnestly trying to understand where you are coming from. And it keeps the pressure of conversation off my shoulders, which is an appreciated bonus.

I associate this level of understanding with my personality and experience of introversion – someone who is caught up in thoughts and daydreams ninety per cent of the time. Because I hyper fixate on things that I hear, see and experience, I feel that I have a more natural sense of understanding in most situations. If not a full understanding, then at the least a relatively detailed one regarding why a person has done what they have.

My initial reaction to what someone shares with me is to mentally place myself in their situation, or to find a way to relate through similar experiences of my own – which I have had many a moment to contemplate, believe me. I make myself understand as best I can, to support them as best I can – and the way my mind works, accompanied by my empathetic inclination, allows me to do so.

I acknowledge that when it comes to my own situations, I tend to assume too much on too little evidence. While some of my assumptions are correct (solid intuition in this gut of mine), there are equally some that are not. What can I say, I'm human and my observation skills are flawed and cannot be solely relied upon. I recognize that communicative interaction is required to truly be there for someone and in those times, I don't mind it so much. The best any of us can do is lend a listening ear and ask what it is that person needs to feel heard.

So, when I am quiet and seemingly disconnected amongst the bustle of conversation, know that I am simply attempting to internally process everything; ensuring I understand and can compose an appropriate response. If I don't respond at all, or for an awkwardly long period of time, know that my mind is probably overwhelmed by the intense overthinking of figuring out if, and where, I can fit into the conversation - not something my degree taught me. Occasionally, even the hyper-awareness of the total time elapsed prevents me from just saying something which, in my experience, has required elaboration to smooth things over within some relationships.

Remember those 'hundreds of conversations' I have in my head on a daily basis? How I wish this were hyperbolic. Anyway. When this happens within a physical interaction, it's usually my way of understanding what is being said and where the conversation would go if I had to reply with one of my many response options. Unfortunately, in serious conversations this doesn't exactly help to lighten the mood or move past the issue. I will dissect every word to figure out what the communicator has said, what they are trying to say and what the underlying messages are in context to their physical demeanour. Then I consider replying and imagine what the communicator's possible response would be to the considered reply, determining where I would rather steer the conversation. Imagine a *Multiverse of Madness* in your mind; simultaneously considering every possible route of communication, exhausting right? Now, the problem with this is that 10 minutes have gone by and the person I am talking to has already added to what they originally said… which leaves me with more conversational gymnastics to perform quickly and quietly in my mind.

No wonder they feel frustration towards me because, yeah, they may as well be talking to a wall. Am I offended by this? Somewhat. Can I blame them? Hardly. In their defence, there is no way they can possibly understand what is happening in my mind (as if I even understand it), and all they have to go on is my blank expression, rogue tears and fidgety fingers.

I am just as frustrated with myself for not opening my mouth and saying *something* to indicate my eager involvement in the conversation when this overwhelm hits. I get so caught up in my thoughts of how I can change, resolve, or constructively contribute to the conversation that reality becomes distorted, and I make more of a mess of things.

Eventually, when I do start talking and bring up the responses that were highlighted in my mental mayhem, the conversation is either poorly saved or deemed irrelevant by that point. You can trust that for hours later (more likely for the next few days) I will repetitively mull over the entire ordeal and think of everything I should have said and how I could have responded from the start to save us all many a frustration.

What an introvert's quiet communication comes down to is reckless thought patterns and calculated speech. We focus on how to correctly word a sentence (once we've filtered a decent response), which inflections to place on which words, and how all the ways of speaking a specific sentence aloud could be interpreted. We desperately don't want to be misunderstood by what we say – it can be embarrassing or detrimental to a relationship (equal fears for me as an introvert) – yet we are often misunderstood anyway thanks to our nonverbal thought process.

Occasionally, even our movements are calculated to offset our words and it will take a few vocal gasps of air before our vocal cords vibrate and deliver our brain's message.

As much as people should try to understand that sometimes we need time before we can reply, introverts should try telling the people we're talking to that we are listening but need time to process… two to five working days would be ideal, but we will make do with a minute (or ten).

On a serious note, introverts should try to accept and acknowledge their thought process while realising their physical environment. As an introvert, I know it's difficult. The goal of this activity is to bring yourself towards yourself, to attempt to control your thoughts pre- or mid-spiral and to allow the person you are with to accept and acknowledge your thought process too. I remind myself that I am capable of conversing and choose to prioritise my relationship with a person over my fear of embarrassment, being misunderstood or pending disappointment. Do I always remind myself of these things? Of course not, I love a pity party as much as the next introvert. But I am working on it.

All I am saying, is that having these types of conversations with the people in our lives (the important ones anyway), will reduce the risk of misinterpretation of our behaviour and lead to more constructive conversations for all parties involved. Remember to verbally acknowledge their side of the conversation and ask for some time to process if you need it – just be realistic about the time people can give you in the midst of a conversation, don't take advantage of the opportunity to spiral further or procrastinate broaching an uncomfortable conversation (yes, I know we do this, but we need to not, okay?).

Pathetically Empathetic

Erlebnisse

The experiences, positive or negative, that we feel most deeply and through which we truly live.

When you spend a fair amount of time imagining yourself in and out of a variety of situations, you can develop a deep sense of empathy towards others. You might not have lived the same experiences as someone, but you can mentally place yourself in their shoes and empathetically feel for them in their circumstance.

I consider myself a pathetically empathic introvert because I find myself in the shoes of others quite regularly (daily) and in almost every circumstance. When I watch a movie (even a corny, clichéd, painful to watch movie), I quickly tune into the emotions of the characters – happy or sad. Honestly, happier moments trigger me more easily because I just feel so darn happy for and with them; joy is an incredibly strong emotion. Reality TV's golden buzzers and chair turns are literally too much for me and, depending on who's around, I either leave the room to sob or stare at the ceiling to coax the tears back into my eyeballs. I am also drawn to the occasional reality drama series which, sorry for Andrew, turns me into a drama-llama who hyper focuses on every little thing because I'm caught up in the hurt or frustration of the nonsense entertainment I consume.

I have a few examples of how this translates into real life, starting with the time I went to a friend's wedding. Picture it, a beautiful forest clearing, the wind was rushing through the trees above, I was sitting at the far back, away from the couple, who chose to say their vows privately to one another without the microphone - I couldn't hear a word they were saying - but simply watching them react to each other's words had me bawling my eyes out. Having had my own wedding, I could understand the emotions this couple would have been feeling and the pure love and joy shared between them was tangible (to me anyway). I had no choice, thanks to my independently operated mind and body, but to share in it with them – emotions first. More recently I was a bridesmaid for my sister-in-law at her wedding. I was stifling sobs while tears poured out my eyes the whole way down the aisle (yes, before the bride even walked in! And when she did, you know your girl was a blubbering bridesmaid). Weddings always get me – at least once, but on average about three cries for sure.

I both love and not-so-much-love this trait of mine. Being an introvert, I deliberately try not to draw attention to myself, but I can only imagine what people must think about me (which I obviously do) when I sit there with silent tears streaming steadily down my face. At least a wedding provides somewhat of an excuse, but what explanation does one give when one's at home watching TV with the family and the advertisement for a cooldrink sets you off?

Or, how about when you're at a hip-hop competition with a hall filled with people and dancers cheering each other on, clapping, shouting compliments, and supporting their friends and family on stage? Amongst groups of kids in full costume, dancing to heavy bass beats, rap and pop music remixes; there I sat watching my cousin's team dance their hearts out and I couldn't even let out an exuberant 'whoooo' because my voice would catch, and I would choke up because I was so damned proud and I could feel how proud her and the team must've been. The same thing happened at my mother's graduation, my sister's student film screening, and whenever I caught myself in a moment of worship, singing with my dad who was playing guitar and my brother on the drums. It also happened the moment Ally sang on stage for the first time in *A Star is Born*, clearly sentimentality is not a requirement for empathy.

To watch other people achieving a dream or reaching a goal makes me emotional because I can feel the joy and excitement with them. And if they're not the emotional type, then you can bet I'm emotional enough for the both of us, which is the case for me and my emotionally nonchalant paramedic husband. I'm quick to feel happy, proud, sad, angry or heartbroken with a friend, a stranger and even a well-scripted fictional character because I feel their emotions with them. My empathetic nature allows me to, at the best of my ability, understand what they're going through. If I've felt their emotions through my own experiences – and it's highly likely that I have felt them all – I do an emotional recall when I witness a similar experience. Like the saying 'walk a mile in my shoes', I feel I've walked many miles when it comes to empathy.

I may be shy and prefer solitude at times, but people are important to me. It's a delicate balance to strive for. What you need to understand about most introverts, is that we don't have the world of friends. You'll find that once you are our friend it's likely we will remain friends until the end of time. Making new friends is difficult, but in my case, I'm blessed to have a husband who makes friends easily and is willing to share them with me. I'm also lucky that he has great taste in people, and I can happily say that I have built some strong relationships with 'our' friends.

Regardless of my level of friendship with someone, if we are friends I will feel very deeply for – and with – you. There's not much

I wouldn't do for a friend in their time of need. I am ready to drop everything to be there for them and share the burden of their pain or celebrate their joy. And it's only because I'm 'pathetically empathetic' that I can do that. I won't willingly put myself in overly social or uncomfortable situations, but I will for my friends if that's what they need. My usual introverted offer is to be a shoulder to cry on or someone to vent to because that doesn't require much talking on my part. Although, you can trust that by the time I arrive at a friend's place, I have thought a great deal about what I could possibly say to provide comfort. This also adds to my empathetic abilities. By listening and processing people's information, I can place myself in their headspace and try to offer help through my interpretive perspective of their events – quiet communicator, remember?

My empathetic arsenal is also built from the experiences of others who have gone through similar events and shared their stories with me. With this already processed information and the addition of any new insights, I create a library of perspectives that I can access as needed. I have been told that I'm mature for my age (when I was a bit younger at least), and I believe that my empathy is the reason why. My ability to feel deeply as if it were my own experience, to process and relive an event through a friend's account, inadvertently adds to my life's experience and perhaps makes it seem like I know more than I actually do. I don't claim to have much life experience at all to be honest. I think the contributing factor is that I *feel* more than I know, and emotions are powerful things.

Introverts spend more time trying to *interpret* pieces of information than on any other aspect of communication, which holds both a strength and a weakness. The strength is the incredible fountain of empathy unlocked from moments of deep contemplation and imagination. The weakness is the incredible amount of time spent in the mind; exhausting the reserves of mental energy required in any attempt to comfort or respond to a friend in need. Ultimately, it's a matter of finding true understanding: an effort of wanting to understand what someone I care about is going through. This makes me rather protective of my friends since I know what they have gone through, and I feel as though I have shared in a portion of their hardships because I chose to be there for them.

Not everyone understands or considers the other side of the story, which is unfair. It's not difficult to find a quote about being kind towards others because you don't know what battles they're fighting, or not to judge a book by its cover when you haven't truly interpreted the content. But it seems to be difficult for people to change their behaviour and live in accordance with those quotes. Not so much so when you're an introvert who considers what other people think of you on a daily basis, however. For me it's a little easier.

I don't think it's not uncommon for introverts to be empaths. To be an empath is to explore empathy on a deeper level and take on others' emotions, more than just being empathetic and feeling *for* them; we feel *with* them. I spend so much time introspectively imagining myself in likely and unlikely scenarios - for example, when I sit in the back of the car headed out with family and my brain decides to wander, thinking, 'if we were to have an accident right now how would that play out? Who could I protect? Would me trying to physically protect them put them at a higher risk of injury? How would we cope with those who we lose?' Sometimes I do this to such a degree that it affects my reality. As empaths, our moods might change, we might shed a tear or two, or we might smile out of seemingly nowhere.

Our empathy is a strength that speaks to our character. Granted, the uncontrollable tears during a video game cut-scene may seem unnecessary, but it shows how tuned in we are to human emotion, which is critical in social interactions and building relationships. Empathy could be interpreted as weak, over-emotional, or too sympathetic by those who maybe don't understand empathy or are unable to process emotions the same way as we do. Negative insinuations, but honestly, I would rather feel everything all the time. I am a better human because of my empathy.

To use empathy as a segue, allow me to introduce the term 'highly sensitive'. Let me start by saying that not all introverts are highly sensitive people and vice versa. Nonetheless, due to the nature of introverted personality traits, many could be. I definitely am. As a highly sensitive person, I'm incredibly empathetic - I frequently feel most emotions deeply and am sensitive to overstimulation from my external environment – this goes beyond being empathetic for me. To fully immerse myself in the emotion of another speaks to high sensitivity. As for overstimulation – too much socialising within a week, the TV volume turned up too loudly, large crowds or sudden changes in temperature set my nerves a little on edge.

There are many books on the subject of high sensitivity, I recommend you look into them if you are, or suspect you may be highly sensitive and unsure of how to accept and work with it. Like introversion, it's not a dirty word or something to try to rid yourself of. We are all complex beings, the best we can do is learn more about ourselves.

As frustrating as it is to know that your reaction within a certain setting may seem an overreaction compared to others', you shouldn't feel embarrassed about it. My husband will often look over at me when watching something to see if I am, indeed, crying over it again. And then we will laugh about it – well he shakes his head and feigns exasperation and I laugh because I know I can't help it despite how small the trigger may be. I can appreciate the humour in these moments, but I don't disregard my empathetic ability for a second because I know how special it is to be able to feel as others do. It even helps me better understand my own emotions when I subconsciously react to something, which helps me communicate better within my relationships.

If I allowed myself, I could become overwhelmed by the emotions stirred up in me from scripted or real-life situations that play out in front of me. Most of the time I hide the welling eyes or swallow the sob that threatens to escape – I know people won't understand, especially if I don't quite understand what has brought it on. But when I am alone and able to immerse myself in the emotion evoked, I let it take over for as long as my body needs to experience and release it. I don't know if this is considered a healthy behaviour, but if I haven't cried in a while – we all need a cathartic cry every now and then, especially for no reason – I purposefully watch something super sad or joyful to allow myself that emotional release (Disney movies are my go-to). And after a week of overthinking day in and day out, my mind needs it, whether something happened to warrant it or not.

Coming to understand your empathic abilities, empathetic disposition, or high sensitivity, if you possess these qualities, is a positive step toward embracing it as a strength within you. One you can use to improve your relationships and give allowances to yourself in moments you just don't understand – like when an intense feeling of grief washes over you out of the blue. Being an empath can take its toll; learn to name that emotion, feel it, understand where it is coming from, and find an outlet to release it. So, as much as I have referred to myself as 'pathetically empathic', it's not that pathetic at all. Empathy is incredible, and so are you.

Anxiety For Africa

Atychiphobia

Fear of failure, fear of not being good enough.

There are many people who suffer from anxiety, myself included. And while each person's anxieties differ - from the degree of physical effects to the elements that cause it - I will share a few personal anxieties and how my mind plays beautiful games that tend to make matters worse.

Before I begin, it's important to note that there is no such thing as a 'silly' anxiety. You might think it silly to stress about certain things that seem to come more naturally to others but knowing that doesn't necessarily relieve you of that anxiety.

Personally, I have underplayed my anxieties for a long time because I know there are people who have it worse and who require intervention to treat their anxiety. But that doesn't mean that our 'silly' anxieties aren't real or something that needs to be dealt with. Side note: I have since tried therapy and recommend we all do – 'we' as in humans not 'we' as in introverts. We, humans, need to understand our anxiety before we can begin to deal with it, and should never downplay the effects it has on us. Okay? Good, moving on.

I have a deep fear of failure and rejection. Most, if not all, of my anxieties stem from this. What if I mess up at work? What if no one laughs at my incredibly funny joke? What if I look stupid? What if I sound stupid? What if my marriage fails because of something I say? What if no one reads this book? What if people read it and think it's boring? What if people think I'm rude when I'm just not a morning person? For the longest time this fear has been something I've carried with me in *everything* I do including what some may consider to be the simplest of tasks. It's my motivation to remain quiet or soft-spoken and overthink every possible conversational route while speaking to someone. Feeling embarrassed is one of the worst, yet sometimes inevitable, experiences for me. I don't want to look like an idiot in anything I have to do so I would rather not do anything instead.

In high school I took the bus to and from school every day. Not once in five years did I ever take the late bus. Meaning, I never did any after school activities that would require me to stay late and catch the five o' clock evening bus. Why? Well, I didn't know if the bus would pick me up at the usual spot – the school fields were in a different area and the prospect of walking there in the first place was anxiety-inducing for me. It was a smaller bus, which meant I would likely end up sitting next to someone – more anxiety – and I never wanted to risk missing the bus home – anxiety-inducing and potentially parent-displeasing. If there was something I did have to do after school, it was probably compulsory, and I would arrange for my parents to pick me up or stay over by a friend who lived closer to school.

The thought of the late bus routine was enough to work me up and keep me from participating in many school activities. Do I regret missing out? To be honest, not really - if I were to consider attending the social event itself, it would present new anxieties. What I do regret is allowing that anxiety to overtake my decision-making before at least trying it once.

My fear of embarrassment tags along when I meet up with friends; yes, people I'm comfortable with. I don't like walking into a new place (even one I know quite well) without knowing exactly where my person is. I usually message from the car to find out where they are sitting to avoid walking in and looking like a lost puppy while being waved down from right under my nose. It may seem an irrational thing to be embarrassed by, I mean literally no-one cares, but there's nothing like a meetup to accelerate my heart, flush my cheeks and break a sweat. As much as I love to explore new places, the anxiety that comes with it keeps me home most days.

In my present, adulting world, I have encountered many new and very real anxieties. I spoke about eye contact being difficult for introverts (see: me), now can you imagine how problematic this can be in a job interview? And because I am so aware of how important it is to exude confidence and impress your potential employer, I force myself to lock eyes. If my heart wasn't beating dangerously before then, you can be sure it now verges on explosion. To detract from the anxiety I'm feeling, I tend to fidget with my hands - anything to offset the neurons firing in my brain telling my eyes to look away. Usually, I settle for the space between the eyes (it's called compromise).

Fidgeting is one of my physical responses to anxiety. I use it to deflect the anxious energy from my body as an unconscious coping mechanism. My fidgets are either in the form of a restless leg, pinching myself, playing with my nails (the tick-tick sound nobody enjoys), ripping the skin off the side of my fingers, tearing skin off my lips or - my favourite go-to – biting the inside of my cheeks. As much as anxiety affects my mental health, my means of expelling it from my body can also be harmful. Not to mention gross and unflattering.

My body has become so used to resorting to one of these outlets that I hardly notice it anymore - until my husband, friend or family member tells me to "stop chewing your cheeks". Most of the time with Andrew this is usually followed by "what's wrong?" because he knows it's a sign of stress and anxiety. I realise that I have formed a bad habit too, so when I am called out for it, it helps bring me back from wherever my mind has spiralled to. Then I can figure out if there is a stressor to manage or if it's just my subconscious that has taken control and set me on autopilot. But the greatest physical effect of my anxiety are fast, heavy heartbeats.

Going to the gym is difficult for me, it can be a prime spot for embarrassment if you don't know how to use equipment or are surrounded by people confident in their fitness regime. So, I really appreciated when my mother said we could gym together. We created somewhat of a routine: a combination of attending classes and following app-guided workouts. One day, my mom said she couldn't make it. 'Okay,' I told myself, 'you've done this enough times with her before to complete today's session alone'. I talked myself into still going, knowing that my heart was greeting every thought of it with heavy throbs. I got to the gym, went to change, and as I stepped out of the bathroom stall my 'resting' heart rate was up to 120 beats per minute. I was shaking, managing shallow breaths, and on the verge of tears. I stepped onto the treadmill to warm up (the first machine in my sights as I exited the changing room), but quickly phoned my mom to beg her to come because I was freaking out and couldn't gym on my own. Bless her, she joined me and I finished the session as if nothing happened.

My fear of embarrassment not only stopped me from working out alone (for fear of messing up) but kept me from simply leaving (for fear of people realising I only walked in to change before walking out). The one time I went to a gym session on my own, and wasn't completely overwhelmed, was for the five a.m. class – I was too tired to register anything, let alone start overthinking.

It does get better though, and there are many factors that can make your gym experience as an anxious introvert easier. After we got married, we moved to a small town with one locally owned and operated gym, which was a better gym experience for me. You learn the faces, are introduced to the equipment and it helped to go with Andrew most days. I was finally finding myself more comfortable in a gym environment.

We are not forever enslaved by our anxieties or the effects they have on us, but not without some acknowledgment and intervention from our part at least.

It's important to share your anxious tells and anxiety triggers with friends and family. You need them to understand what it means when you phase out of reality, stare into the void, or shake the table because you can't keep your legs still. When your support system misinterprets your signs of anxiety, they can't support you the way that you need them to. To them it may be a pet peeve or annoying habit you've unconsciously formed, which can also be true, but they are missing the root cause of your actions.

Anxiety being misinterpreted and mishandled leads to a defensive person who now feels dismissed and misunderstood on top of everything else. But it's not your loved ones' fault - no one can read minds or understand our ticks without having us provide an explanation or reaching out with what we need first. And though you may not want to because it proves extremely difficult for you, an explanation is always necessary – at least the first time, after that, feel free to be understandably upset.

Open communication in close relationships is so important for longevity of the relationship. The communicative block will remain solid without taking the time and strength to talk it out with your loved ones so that the future of those relationships, and your mental health, may thrive. It's better to face one moment of discomfort talking about real things than it is to be constantly misunderstood and misinterpreted, I promise.

Change is bound to make anyone a little anxious. The most significant change in my life has been getting married, followed by moving to a new home after living in the same house for 24 years. My first thoughts were the usual, 'will there be a female doctor?' – yes, one; 'who will I go to for waxing appointments?' – no-one, I re-friended ye old faithful razor; 'how will I make new friends?' – I won't, luckily my family-in-law live 730 metres down the road; 'what will the church be like?' – like a church, except my first attempt to attend was welcomed with an unexpected human interaction that completely overwhelmed me and I never returned; and 'what will I do all day?' – play housewife because content-creation and digital marketing companies aren't in small towns. It's been over a year now and I'm relatively settled in my small town.

We visit my parents frequently enough to satisfy my craving for shopping malls, coffee dates with friends, going to the church I grew up in, and seeing my family of course. As for work, I applied to multiple online and freelance jobs to try stay within my field and only had a breakthrough 10 months in. While this was rather discouraging, it did allow me to work on my homemaking skills which, previously non-existent, turned out to be just above average. I have yet to produce something completely inedible and, to me, that's a win.

I still experience anxiety when I head into town alone. If I have an appointment or something out of the ordinary to do, my husband supportively goes with me, specifically if it's my first time – grateful barely begins to cover it. There are certain areas of town I don't feel comfortable venturing into alone and I haven't made new friends, but with my family-in-law around I've managed quite well. I thank God that we all love each other and get along, it's one of my biggest blessings. Mostly my anxiety still stems from that rooted fear of embarrassment, from having to make small-talk conversation to familiar faces, and that looming feeling that everyone in town knows who I am, but I have no clue who they are, which happens when you're in the town your husband grew up in, where his dad teaches at the high school and mother manages the hardware store.

Now, if I struggled with this move - a mere 119 km distance from where I grew up - you can imagine how anxious I was about the prospect of moving overseas. To a foreign country where English is not the home language nor Christianity the national religion (culture-shock and premeditated anxiety right there). There are still a few months before proper planning and preparing begin, so I try not to think about it too much. I've already had a breakdown about not taking Koda with us, luckily it's terrible enough for my brain to shove the idea of immigrating almost completely out of my mind... almost, you and I both know I've already over-thought about it – and fleeting thoughts count, especially when there are hundreds fleeting by every half hour.

I will say, what my introversion does help me with is adapting. Once I set up a routine and become more comfortable in my environment, I'm pretty easy going. But it does take a while to settle – you know, healthily where I don't stay cooped up inside the house all day and pretend like I'm happy to do everything from my couch (which I can be but know I shouldn't). To adapt though, I need to do it at my own pace, with tiny little anxious steps that may seem futile to others, but I know will get me there – to that uncomfortable spot right on the edge of my comfort zone.

So, how does an anxious introvert deal with big life changes when they rely on stability and familiarity to function in everyday society? I might have to write another book if I figure that out. In the meantime, I do my best to manage my anxiety. And while I'm no expert, there are a few things that work for me.

Firstly, I think logically about my fear and anxiety. If it's about something I've done (successfully) before, I home in on that experience and remember how it 'wasn't actually that bad' so, technically, I can do it again. Secondly, I purposefully step outside my comfort zone (now and then and in my own time) to put that adaptability into practice - it takes some planning, and a few (or five) failed attempts before I can leave the car, have a solo coffee date, make that phone call (let's all agree right now: email is easier), and fulfil my appointments. Thirdly, and most importantly, I rely on my support system. If I know there's something I need to do, but am actively eluding, I ask someone to join me. It makes me feel small and embarrassed to have to ask, but because it's people I love and trust, I know they won't judge me and we can laugh about it afterwards.

It's important not to rush yourself if you know it's going to cause a panic attack or overwhelm you to the point of unenjoyment.

Don't, however, allow your anxieties and fears to hold you back when you know (and you know that you know) it is a possible feat for you to achieve. No matter what methods you need to rely on – do what works for you.

Dear friends, family, and fellow introverts; don't undermine a person's anxieties. You may not understand why a large gathering comprised of people someone knows freaks them out but respect the fact that it does and ask if or how you could help them through it. Also, understand that what may seem consoling to you, won't necessarily be a comfort to the anxious. Mental health is unique and personal, and one isn't always seeking an outsider's advice on 'how to get over it'. Learn about their fears, the methods and therapies they've tried, and what it is they truly need from a support system.

The more you understand – and introverts; the more you share – the easier it is to empathise and assist your fearful friends, even if that means simply leaving them alone for a while. It's not personal, sometimes we just need our space to think and recharge. There is *so much* that goes on in that busy mind of ours, strategically masked behind a this-is-my-okay-face visage. A willingness to understand and an open heart to share are the two sides of a beautiful conversation-sandwich.

Deep Feels

Ineffable

Too great or extreme to be expressed or described in words.

A deep feeler can easily be connected to introverted, anxious, and/or highly sensitive individuals. The combination of time spent in our minds, our empathetic ability, and the littlest of things that worry us, lead us to feel more emotional than most. 'Pathetically Empathetic' covered this too, but don't be fooled, just because we feel an emotion deeply doesn't mean we can articulate it through words or actions. Accept, even without complete understanding, that people who feel emotions deeply, can be difficult to read.

Personally, I try to 'keep face' in public, or when in the presence of someone other than my husband. There's not much I can keep from my man - even his birthday surprises are rather unsurprising. I don't want people to know if something is wrong, but if someone should ask and break through my 'I'm fine', or 'it's okay' response shields, I usually open up or, more commonly, break down. The worst is when I'm not even sure why I feel sad, angry, frustrated, drained or just 'off'. It could be from stewing in thoughts about something that's happened, or been said in passing, that my mind spirals around instead of letting go – it doesn't have to be immediately relevant to affect me.

My guess is, we feel so deeply because we constantly focus on dissecting and understanding our feelings throughout the day – what *exactly* we are feeling may elude us and the longer we spend exploring it, the deeper we fall into it. I rarely discover the root cause of my emotions, despite mulling over them all day long, and letting them roam unfiltered – not great for those with me during that time.

I like to do this thing where I create ideal feelings for certain situations. Basically, as I play out a scenario in my mind – exactly how I would like it to go and how I would counter any possible deviations – I hold on to that created emotion and experience. I count it as proactive happiness, but it usually turns out to be more of a predetermined mini depression. You see, when something happens in real life that was not part of my favourable, envisioned scenario, I tend to take it personally... within myself.

To set these expectations is to set yourself up for failure – something I've come to learn yet still struggle, or forget, to apply. One ends up caught in their thoughts and how they want to feel instead of living in the moment and understanding how they are actually feeling. As complicated as this may be for you (the person experiencing emotions), can you imagine how the people around you feel when you have this internal struggle going on and they're just trying to find out how your week was? People cannot read minds, unfortunately, and if we introverts take our thoughts and expectations personally to the people we care about, we cannot be offended. They, in turn, can be defensive and upset about our out-of-context behaviour. It may be an internal struggle, but it has external effects that carry over into our interactions and immediate environment. For example, I find myself deep in the feels and trying to compensate by thinking my way into a neutral mood while Andrew is trying to connect with me. But, because I'm so distracted, he starts to feel frustrated and ignored and I start to feel irritated because he doesn't understand that I'm trying to fix myself – of course without me sharing that I am currently working through something. The answer is no, it's not supposed to make sense.

As frustrating as this paradox is, it can be a necessary process for us introverts. I have to think hard about what and why I'm feeling a certain emotion to move through it – even though it affects my mood and interactions within my relationships. If I don't figure it out, I know that emotion will consume me until I become someone no-one would enjoy being around (including myself). The paradox lies in the fact that by overthinking to try and figure it out, it consumes me anyway. Usually, I try to find and follow the criminal trail of emotional-evidence that led to this point... Spoiler – they're mostly self-inflicted crimes – those darned expectations. But once I have made my ruling on the matter, I can 'bring myself towards myself', as Andrew often reminds me, and summon up my apologies to those caught in the crossfire of my deep feels. And if there is no opportune moment to apologise, I have a little pity party and move on from it.

Common emotions that trigger this kind of downward spiral include embarrassment, offense, and joy. The possibility of me offending someone is worse than if I am the offended – that just makes me more reserved. If I am embarrassed by even the slightest of miscommunications, I'll be miserable.

One evening playing cards with Andrew's family, I was asked to take a photo of them drinking a shooter, so I did. I expected them to pose, but they took the shot, so I quickly tried to take burst photos as it was too late to switch to video, which I thought was the better option in the first place, but I heard 'photo', so I took a photo. Afterwards they looked through the photos and my husband simply commented '*Ai, Liefie,* why didn't you take a video?' And I switched off like a light; no longer wanting to sit and play while everyone had a good time – not even a little concerned

bothering us, or what to do to get out of this slump on our own –
especially when we want to be alone. I find it's usually a culmination
of the week's interactions that drain me emotionally. And not
necessarily all negative; it could range from an interaction with a
friend, a stranger, a drive-by comment from a loved one, a clumsy
moment in public or having isolated myself for three days in a row.

Point is, it's not always easy to instantly recognise and
manage one's triggers and work through the deep feelings we're
experiencing. Sometimes the right thing to do is wait it out and let
us get over it ourselves. If it's minor it may only take a few hours to
resolve, but if it has been brewing, prepare for a day (or a few) of a
'not yourself' spouse, partner, friend, sibling, child, colleague, or
person.

Allowing your emotional drainage to render you down to
being terrible company isn't healthy. My fellow introverts – you
know what it feels like when you start shutting down for as-of-yet-
undiscovered reasons. When you notice that, verbalise what you
need or excuse yourself to feel the feelings and process in ways that

work for you. Loved ones of introverts – yes, it can be frustrating to not know how to cheer us up. Believe me, we're just at frustrated for not knowing the who, what, why and when of our 'moments'. What would be helpful, aside from not projecting extra frustration, is offering us a space to verbalise, or simply be, while we process. Communication is always the key to avoiding misinterpretations. Even communicating that you need a few minutes before you can talk about anything is beneficial to both parties.

And just that small step in communication could be the healthiest decision you make for your mental health as well. I won't speak for all introverts on this, but this is deeply personal, like most things in this book, and I have only ever shared this with very few people. With the mental health struggles that my introversion, anxiety, an overactive imagination, and high sensitivity bring, one could imagine the overwhelm becoming too much. When I deal with something intense (internally of course), there is a train of thought that comes through almost every time. What if coincidentally, accidentally, I was to die right now instead? Not by suicide but considering how convenient dying could be at a time of struggle or when I've hurt someone else. Like if I were to have an accident – lose control of my car, choke on my food, be bitten by something venomous – anything that would take my life without inconveniencing or harming anyone else.

I wouldn't harm myself, just kind of, desperately, wish for something to happen to ease the burden that I feel I am in that moment. It's a cop out, I realise that and when I share those thoughts with Andrew, he pulls me out of that train of thought. I know my heart is not serious about coincidentally, accidentally, taking my life, but the fact that my mind goes there (sometimes too quickly) when I fail or let others down is a problem. Once again highlighting the importance of sharing, open communication and taking control of your moments so that they don't take control of you.

We all have an activity, conversation, person, book – something – that drains our emotional batteries. For introverts, I think there are a lot more potential emotional drainers than for others, considering all we overthink and feel. One of the main conditions that send me down a 'meh' spiral is socialising. It's one of the dominant indicators that you may be an introvert – your energy is depleted because of an overcharged social calendar, not a Vitamin D deficiency (although, it could be both). Look, I love being with my friends, occasionally going out, and generally having a great time with those who are close to me. I love weekends away with friends or family, but I will need a moment to have a 'moment' beforehand, possibly during, and definitely afterwards.

Socialising can be exhausting for introverts, I trust that this is easier to understand now that you know a bit more about what goes on in our minds. How we can overthink every verbal or nonverbal cue towards us so as not to misunderstand or be caught off-guard and embarrassed. Our difficulty to maintain appropriate eye contact within a conversation. The realm of possibilities that arise from being the centre of attention when asked a question. Our anxiety to speak aloud and hope no-one rejects what we have to say. The hyper-awareness of our physical environment, how we fit into it; and the people around us. Pulling the skin on our fingers until we start to bleed from steadily becoming overwhelmed by our social and environmental interactions. Our empathetic investment into every person's story. How we feel every emotion a thousand times more than the average human should…

Give me a minute, I need a 'moment'.

People Pleaser

Firgun

The act of sharing in or even contributing to someone else's pleasure or fortune, with a purely generous heart and without jealously; or of sharing credit fairly.

I think this is a good time to talk about the people-pleasing trait. We've established that embarrassment, rejection, and fear of failure are our 'day-jackers'. They are also the reason why people pleasing is important to us introverts. Due to my lack of self-assurance and self-appreciation, I want people to genuinely like me and be impressed by me, which often leads me to be a pushover and someone who struggles to say no. I could probably count on one hand the number of times I have said no to someone because I didn't want to do something.

Why would I want to upset someone by telling them no, even if it means I may compromise myself in the process?

I am not an ingenuine person. I don't think I am anyway. I'm aware of the different sides of my personality I embrace depending on the scenario or who I talk to. But if we're being honest, we all do this to some degree. The way I interact with my husband and family is different to that with my friends. Mostly because I worry my friends will see the real me and not want to hang out anymore, you know, because I'm such a weirdo. Although, at some point in all my close friendships, this weirdo comes out anyway and my friends usually reciprocate with their own this-is-me-being-very-comfortable-with-you side. Again, this *real* side of me and the *other* side I initially present, are both genuine sides of my personality. I am a shy introvert; of course I will be more polite, reserved, and soft-spoken upon first meeting me – because that's who I am. But I can also be more confident, verbal, and hilarious when I want to be. My default is to choose a pleasing persona while I make new connections and read the emotional environment.

People rarely put their entire selves on display from the start. I need to feel comfortable with someone before I feel I can be my truest self - I don't want to be judged and I need to know that I can trust them. By trust, I mean that they won't make me feel even more self-conscious about my introversion, which could send me into a self-deprecating spiral that will consume my thoughts for the rest of our interaction and likely days to come.

This doesn't mean the initial impression I offer is dishonest, it's just a filtered version of myself, if that makes sense? If you were to ask people who really know me, they would say I'm not the same person they first met - I am more vocal with a killer sense of humour – I consider any opportunity to pull out a pun the epitome of humour, just so you know.

Generally, upon first meeting me I don't have too much to say and rather embrace the role of a good listener. People I meet through (and with) people I am already comfortable with, however, encounter my 'full-me state' and question that I'm a shy, introverted individual who comes across as stand-offish.

My need to be liked makes up for my minimal interaction because it allows me to get maximum validation for my personality type. What does that mean? Well, in my mind, it means that I can get people to like me (as an introvert) if I remain neutral in conversation and display a neutral, pleasing demeanour. It might not make sense to you, but it makes things okay in my brain and helps me feel less uncomfortable in unknown social situations.

I am friendly, but it doesn't always come across when I withdraw from group conversations and sit with my resting, focused, wallflower face. Yes, I could add to a conversation, but I choose to stay quiet for fear I embarrass myself and damage my first impression. It's my personal social loophole – how can people like, or not like me, if I just remain quiet in my corner? Unfortunately, the answer could very easily be that I just come across as unmemorable.

I acknowledge there are flaws to this personality trait, many of which I've had the opportunity to experience first-hand and learn from. Firstly, not wanting people to have the wrong impression of me, even if it's the right impression. This has made it difficult for me to find and love myself as I would constantly adapt my opinions and jump on the trending bandwagon for my friends, even if I didn't quite agree. It became second nature to temporarily flip a switch to ensure that I retained the relationship and remained likeable. 'I don't know' is my staple people-pleaser phrase to remain neutral; put aside what I really think, how I feel or what I would rather do to ensure the other person feels accommodated. This unsurety is a safety net I throw out to learn their preferences and reel in the ways I could manipulate my response to appease them. Okay, not all the time, sometimes with everything that goes on in my mind I honestly just do not know how I feel or what I want, but can you blame me?

Secondly, staying in relationships or friendships that aren't beneficial to either person involved. I am sure there are many introverts who fight to stay in relationships like this. We hold on to the few people with whom we've managed to be completely vulnerable. The thought of losing someone who holds all your secrets and has the power to play on your fears and hurt you the most, causes incredible anxiety and desperation. In my experience anyway. I was in a four-year relationship before I met my husband. The foundations of which were deceptive and the failures within stemmed from a fear of loss on both our parts. Sit on a sharp object long enough and eventually you'll find it somewhat comfortable. To know it's not going to get better, that this is not what a loving relationship should be, or that you've invested so much time and energy on someone only to lose it all in seconds… it's rough. I didn't want to lose someone so close to me for obvious reasons. But the less obvious reason, conjured from the most imaginative corners of my mind, was that he now held the power to expose me regardless of the truth or the fact that he is not that type of person.

But that's people-pleasing and anxiety for you – taking your worst fears of vulnerability and imagining a scenario into existence, which hurts even more. All because you, an introvert, decided to open up to someone and, try as you may, could not keep them happy, and now you have no influence over how they feel about you anymore. Yes, Tasmin, that's how it works; you have complete control over what and how other people think despite barely having any control over your own mind.

Thirdly, people-pleasing makes it very difficult to say no. You don't exactly learn the importance of saying no either because you're more attuned to the result of what your consistent 'yes' provides to others. You do, however, learn about resentment and self-disappointment from constantly agreeing to things you aren't keen on or don't agree with. But I still say yes when I don't really want to because I'm flattered someone thought of me, which means they like me, which means I need to say yes so that they will keep liking me. See the problem? It is seeking validation for being shy and not really knowing what to do about it, so I ensure at (almost) all costs people enjoy my company regardless.

I acknowledge these issues and how they affect me, and yet, it has taken me so long – too long for me to admit – to do something about it. Today, I still have to actively work on my people-pleasing problems because it's so easy to resort to my 'smile and wave, you can cry about it later'-tactic. Even for small things, like declining an invite for coffee. If I want to simply stay home, have a 'meh' day or recharge from previous social activities, it's important to say no to those too. In fact, it's a good place to practice saying no, especially if you struggle with moral obligation and guilt-tripping yourself into saying yes to all the big things – there's a lot more to unpack there, but that, my friend, is what therapy is for.

Over the years I have learned more about and embraced my values around who I am. I don't momentarily wander away from them anymore, especially not for the sake of simply pleasing someone else's values. If I'm confronted by someone with opposing views and who tries to persuade me, depending on who they are, I either speak up, or (usually) remain silent. I know keeping quiet isn't the best, but it's better than throwing my 'self' out the window. Also, my silence is usually accompanied by an unimpressed look, so they can at least see that I disagree. I'm still working on it; I think I will always be working on it, and baby steps are still steps.

As for people-pleasing to maintain relationships, I don't do much of that anymore either, I am learning from my experiences.

'Realisation' is a difficult concept to accept, let alone in the moment itself. But as difficult as those realisation moments are in relationships; they help us understand our worth and the value of putting in effort where effort is reciprocated and appreciated. I still don't want to offend anyone or embarrass myself so I will always remain friendly, but the people who understand my type of friendship and don't take advantage of me, are the relationships I put equal effort into. I know I'm not the friend who will make plans or message you every day, but I am the friend who is ready to be there for you, the friend with whom, when we do meet up, will seem as if no time has passed.

People-pleasing is not an easy trait to manage with all the aspects that surround it. Choosing yourself above others also doesn't come naturally to me, neither as a Christian, nor as an introvert. There needs to be a balance of honouring and respecting your boundaries in order to honour and respect yourself. Personally, I know people-pleasing comes easy to me because I struggle with self-esteem and self-confidence. It's easier to berate myself in public and boost someone else's ego than acknowledge my own awesomeness. But I'm working to change that narrative. As an introvert, saying no is difficult. Letting go of close relationships is terrifying. Voicing your own opinion seems worthless. But saying no is important. Having people who love and understand you, *as you are*, is freeing. And standing up for yourself is inspiring. I try to strive towards the more positive end of the spectrum.

Alter-Extrovert

Scintilla

A tiny, brilliant flash or spark; a small thing; a barely visible trace.

Excluding social context (which is super influential), in some cases introverts have an extroverted-alter-ego, which may be why people don't always see the introvert upon first meeting me.

My 'alter-extrovert' tends to come out when I'm being competitive – any games-night or challenge thrown my way; when I'm comfortable with friends or family members (social context); on the rare occasion I feel confident in what I am doing (like, blue-moon rare); when I feel safe – usually with my closest network of beautiful souls; when I am the only responsible adult in the room (scary thought); or, when I'm in situations that require people-management to complete a task (so, group work).

While I despise being the centre of attention, if I am placed with people who won't take initiative to do what is required to succeed, I will - subtly, politely, kindly, quietly – assert myself into the leadership role. Generally, I don't consider myself a leader, but I know that, if necessary, I can take control. I don't like to fail, remember? I recognise leadership qualities in my personality, so I know I technically have what it takes… it's just so counterintuitive to my introverted instinct.

I've never really been a team player and not because I'm unable to work with others, I'm just used to doing things on my own. I never played team sports, I did gymnastics, which was individually focused. I like being responsible for my actions and results. I want to know that I earned any validation or constructive criticism for my work. It's part of my improvement process. But team sports and group projects require equal effort from each member and, as we've all likely experienced, it hardly ever happens that way. For reasons of wanting to succeed and not look like a fool, I nominate myself as leader or full load-bearer. I ensure everyone does their set part, help them out if needed, or pick up their slack entirely. In these situations, I quickly assume leadership and get involved in ways that make my inner introvert cringe.

But my alter-ego is something I cannot and do not consciously think about. It either happens in the moment, or it doesn't happen at all – because by then I might've had too much time to overthink it. And this is something that frustrates me; I know I am capable of so many things because there's proof, in the experiences of previous successful outcomes, that I've been able to do it before.

I went to a performing arts college for a year after high school. I initially wanted vocal coaching but was somehow roped into applying for the whole programme, which included singing (cool), musical theatre (like fancy singing right?), dancing (no problem, I have some dance experience) and drama (oh dear). Me, an introvert with no drama background, performing on a stage in front of people, yeah, sure. My drama experience at that point could be summed up in three performances: at-home garage performances for the parents; a quickly thrown-together skit at grade 8 camp where I boldly imitated 'soft and bouncy hair' from *Shrek 2* (super cringe, but also super funny - I was embarrassed by the appropriate laughter and weird confidence I experienced because of it); and a musical production of *Godspel* at my church.

These acting classes included group skits, full productions, and solo improvised performances. Yikes! – If you know me, you know I don't say 'yikes'; it felt *that* bad. My solo 'improv' skits were planned to some extent. I would be given a line (on the spot) to feature in my performance, but I already had different characters and scenarios setup in my mind to work the provided line into. That's probably not how we were supposed to do it but, hey, I had found a method that comforted my introvert. If you were to ask me to perform today, I wouldn't be able to do it. Firstly, it's been almost a decade since. Secondly, there's just no way I'm going to willingly embarrass myself without some type of incentive (like *having* to pass improv class for example). Then again, I know I could do it because I have done it, but that fact alone just isn't enough to persuade me.

If I'm honest, my true, comfortable weirdo self - who I am around my people - can be somewhat extroverted. But also, not entirely. Confused? Same. I think it boils down to my use of humour and confidence to make a fool of myself with family and close friends. Around new people or acquaintances I'm too concerned about what they think of 'basic me' that I don't even consider whipping out my fantastic wit in case they don't get it or it's not as sharp as I consider it to be – I just keep it to myself until I'm home and can recount my thoughts and laugh at myself out loud. My performing arts experience has led to a belief that I could do more of it if I wanted to. But the alter-extrovert is not my entirety, despite being prevalent in my most 'me' state. Don't worry, I'll expand on this further in the chapter.

I consider myself a relatively hilarious person (if that wasn't already obvious). I've surprised, and terrified, myself at how confidently I'm assuring every reader of my hilarity while thinking zero 'laughs while reading' are highly probable. But if I can claim hilarity in a job interview, I think it's safe for me to immortalise it in this book (yes, I really did do that). Point being, when I do make jokes in comfortable company, it's a natural instinct – a well-thought, well-timed, natural instinct – comedic timing is real. If I'm unsure whether my humour will be understood or appreciated, I say it a little quieter, a bit too fast for people to hear properly or start blushing as the words escape my lips. Sometimes I'm asked to repeat one of these doubted jokes, only to receive pity laughs, nothing more than air being forcefully expelled from someone's nose.

Consequently, I'm my own cheerleader and will be the first, and sometimes simultaneously the last, to laugh at something I know is going to be (or supposed to be) funny – and while I'm audibly giggling on the outside you can be sure my inner introvert is crying, dying and regretting her alter-extrovert's faux pas. Side note: I hope you have found and appreciated the traces of funny I've hidden in this book… if not, then I was just kidding, there's no humour here, please keep reading.

Some may say this 'true self' makes me more of an extrovert. But I disagree. My introverted tendencies still apply even when I'm in my alter-extroverted mode. I still become overwhelmed by socialisation, I still require time to recharge, I still prefer to be the quiet listener in the corner instead of the person in control of the conversation. It's not to say that I am two different people, because that's not the case and is, in my opinion, a great misconception about people and personalities in general. Who I am is a culmination of all my genuine personality traits and habits; I believe the same applies to everyone. I wrote a short poem about this concept:

Every side I've shown

Every secret I've shared

Every smile and tear exposed

That is who I am.

That is the real me.

All of it together

Or else I'm no-one at all.

Many introverts have extroverted moments in specific environments and I'm sure extroverts may experience introversion on rare occasions too. I love to sing but hate to be in the spotlight. I was asked to sing at an end-of-year social for a counselling organisation my mom volunteered at. There were less than 20 people present but I was shaking, my mouth dried up on the first note, and I mainly sang to my family's faces and the neon exit sign at the back of the room... which was awkward because it wasn't above anyone's head as the people were seated to my left and right. However, take me to a karaoke bar and put me on stage and I will rock out to whatever song it is I'm singing.

Flashback to my bachelorette singing Shaggy's *It Wasn't Me* with my sister, Amy Winehouse's *Valerie* with the bestie, and Avril Lavigne's *Sk8ter Boi* with all my girls. What a time. Yes, there may have been a bar full of 'liquid courage' at my disposal, but the environment was a safe opportunity for my extroverted self to take the reins while still comfortable enough for my introverted self to handle.

My love for singing and making people smile with my humour gives my inner introvert confidence when I need it. My unique traits allow me to be a perfectly acceptable combination of an introvert and an extrovert, which allows me to satisfactorily operate in general society, albeit an 80:20 ratio. And even if that twenty per cent tends to show up more often than the introverted eighty per cent, introversion is still the dominant part of who I am. I make jokes, but I still overthink them, I spend the night singing in a karaoke bar, but it takes me about a month to recharge before I can consider doing it again. I can take charge of a project and lead, but I'm filled with anxiety throughout, questioning my authority even in situations where the only option was to lead.

I am an introvert who has a few extroverted traits. And I'm glad that I do. I do dissect my extroverted performances – sometimes for weeks – after they've occurred and once my introvert mind regains control. Sometimes, I even feel embarrassed after the fact. Post-bachelorette, I was embarrassed at how I was dancing – the typical in-the-club-swaying-with-awkward-hands, unoriginal-gesturing-to-the-words-you're-singing; and jumping-with-a-fist-pump movements that you're imagining is exactly it – thank you friend who caught this all on camera. At the end of the day, it's nothing I regret because I had so much fun and experienced freedom from my more detrimental introverted tendencies for a few hours. Also, I probably won't ever see that exact crowd of people again, and if necessary, there are other karaoke places out there for me and my friends to conquer. Thank goodness.

A Little Obsessive

Goya

Transporting suspension of disbelief that happens when fantasy is so realistic that it temporarily becomes reality.

There is a limit to how much one's mind can be subjected to before it reaches a breaking point. In my life I believe I have experienced two such moments – and I choose to make a conscious effort to limit it to just those two. (Editing this two years later – yeah, I'm up to three.)

This does not refer to when I shut down, become extremely quiet, or distance myself. I am referring to physical, mental and emotional breaking – sobs, tremors, fleeting thoughts of suicide, hysteria, disbelief, pain, and total overwhelm. Obsessive thinking hyped up by an overactive imagination that leads to paranoia and causes an external reaction to what is being experienced internally.

Disclaimer: this chapter is heavy and deeply personal; I understand if you're not ready to explore these themes, but I encourage you to acknowledge them, if you notice them in yourself, to prevent self-harm or self-destructive behaviour. Know that many people experience these phenomena and that you are stronger than you *think* – because what we *think* tends to be the ingrained, root problem. There are likely many psychological explanations around what I am about to share, but I am purely describing the experiences as they have manifested through my introversive qualities.

It's easy to believe that an introvert can become overwhelmed by their thoughts and imagined realities. Well, with anxiety, hesitation, the need to please, empathy, an emotional disposition, and stereotypical quirks as daily occurrences; overwhelm is almost a default trait to the personality type, right? I readily find myself caught up in thoughts regardless of whether I have a reason to be thinking about anything.

People automatically create associations with words and actions, empowering it by assigning a specific meaning based on their experiences, which usually creates an accompanying emotion. Over the years, I have (naturally and humanly) accumulated an encyclopaedia of emotional associations that, unfortunately, are not all sunshine and joy. Honestly, most of my associations are negative and induce stress related heart aches when stimulated – and not necessarily at the fault of whoever triggered it. In my experience, these associations become little obsessions.

If enough time passes with no negative association run-ins, I obsessively overthink myself into one. I overanalyse every word, emoticon, look, Instagram story, comment, or simply – when I feel for a quick spiral – the lack thereof, creating a scenario that is entirely fictional.

I add meaning to these created situations based on past experiences and try figure out how I have screwed up or how the 'culprit' has targeted this personal attack. An attack I technically know is not possible for some people to assert, as I have not shared my entire life experiences with them, so they wouldn't even know how to intentionally do it.

Regardless, once I start obsessing, everything is personal, and it's almost as if I long for that hurt and attention. In hindsight, the only way I could justify it is as a cry to share or find compassion and love where I feel I didn't have it before. Unfortunately, as you will find from one of my experiences, it seems to cultivate a response effort to hurt them back and make someone feel the way they have made me feel, even when it's just in my mind.

The two moments you will read about happened at two very different times of my life, with two very different people. I share these with you to provide understanding around how an introvert's mind can run away with them, how we (along with many others who suffer from anxiety and other mental health issues) lose control to our emotions and imaginations, and struggle to regain control once the obsessive spiral begins.

The first moment is the association that resulted in the second moment years later. I guess, one's first mental breakdown has to occur (seemingly) out of nowhere before it can become an associated experience.

My ex and I had been together for a while and were okay to keep it that way when this moment occurred. Who we were then, are not who either of us are now, and while the themes of this book have recalled the more unfortunate memories, we both acknowledge responsibility for ending the relationship – we truly experienced growth from our time together. He was older than me and the relationship started as an infatuation, which then led to love and, eventually, a discontent but comfortability of 'us'. It was my first significant relationship, one that allowed us to learn a lot about ourselves and challenge each other creatively. But it was an unhealthy relationship, and I was blind to it. I may wish some things could have been different or avoided, but this relationship has contributed to who I am today, and there is gratefulness in that.

It's possible my associations related to this moment may be mistaken as my memory can be unreliable. However, what I have written is based on my recollection of pivotal events that contributed to my break and which remain true to me mentally and emotionally. Another adverse facet of introversion mind games is holding onto various acts and accumulating them into one giant emotional outburst, usually releasing at an inopportune moment, seeming to simultaneously be about nothing and everything. How lovely.

One contributing event was on a movie date. We started arguing before the movie, I don't remember what about, but I do remember leaving the theatre mid-film. I walked to the entrance of the mall thinking, 'I need to leave. I'll just walk home'. Now, it was dark and knowing anything about South Africa, and being a woman, we all know it was a stupid idea. Standing in the mall parking lot, crying, and contemplating my relationship, I considered the possibility of not being with him, which piqued my anxiety. I went back to the cinema and sat a few rows behind him. It was the first time I considered that maybe we weren't supposed to be together. He was my first, and I was terrified of what it would mean if we weren't together in every context of our relationship.

I thought I was doing something wrong, that I was the reason the relationship would fail. Being hard on yourself is another chink in the introverted armour. And let me tell you, we do it so well. It's kind of like a complimentary trait to people-pleasing that when something fails, it's probably because of us. We chose to be involved so we take responsibility for all of it; obsessing over every action and utterance to *find* that blame in ourselves. It's certainly true for me at least.

We were driving home (either the same night or days later) having another argument when it happened. I had gone quiet and shutdown at this stage when I was told, 'I might as well be talking to a wall' (the fan-favourite phrase) and something along the lines of, 'you must be my punishment for my past'. The word my mind caught, started to dissect and that caused me to start stuttering and muttering it aloud repeatedly - with body shakes and frozen tears – *punishment*. I broke. I could no longer comprehend my environment, hear what was shouted or think about the entire meaning of the word itself. Punishment. It stayed with me throughout the rest of our relationship. It dropped by whenever we argued or whenever he was upset. He may not have meant it as I took it (we all know how high emotions fly during lovers' quarrels), nevertheless, the idea of me qualifying as someone's punishment engraved itself in my mind. The meaning and associations attached.

Hurt only hurts and words may only associate, but words associated *with* hurt, can break the person who has bound themselves to them. Not being enough or even just good for anyone, was drilled into me through that moment. *Punishment* became an instant obsession and association despite apologies and forgiveness. I was so used to obsessing over it and evoking the physical, emotional, and mental effects it had on me that it almost became comfortable. Today, I recognise the damage caused by that relationship. However unintentional, it happened and, as an introvert, I have, of course, thought about it for an unhealthy amount of time. And while I don't actively allow it to have that same power over me, there have been times in my relationship with my husband when *punishment* briefly flashed behind my eyes and evoked fearful heart-thumps. But only for an instant because I know Andrew is his own man, that ours is a different relationship, and that I am stronger than I used to be.

Yes, wounds heal, but they leave scars and scars can itch years after the incident. Obsessive overthinking is kind of like that. Call it a phantom itch if you will, but certain triggers, conscious or not, beckon us to scratch and we can't always help ourselves but to entertain and descend into the self-destructive spiral. I experienced the problems of four relationships in one, from cheating and competing against addiction, to emotional manipulation and verbal abuse. And while it helped me realise what I wanted and needed from a relationship, it affected aspects of my future relationship with my husband.

From the power of associations and the meaning I attached to certain triggers; I can acknowledge that sometimes Andrew falls victim to my moments. Every relationship has disputes, but I found that when I've felt really hurt or offended, it's connected to my associations of those triggers rather than my husband's actions.

When trust became an issue in my previous relationship, my 'gut feeling' was gospel-type truth. And some doubt and gut-feelings I experience with Andrew are attachments to the actions of my ex, which is problematic. So, if something felt familiar with Andrew, I would explain my previous experience, and bring understanding as to why I felt uneasy, emotional, or hurt. Being able to talk to Andrew about these things has been such a blessing, one I do not take for granted. He is incredibly patient and a rock of calm amidst my ramblings and meltdowns. He knows how to bring me back towards myself, into reality instead of further down the spiral. '*Liefie*, you're amazing, I love you.'

Andrew and I were about a month into our first long-distance stint. A 12 000 km stint with no foreseeable end-date and rivalling our longest time spent apart: a pathetic five days. He was in a new country (yes, we did make the move to Qatar), meeting new people, experiencing new things and I was stuck in my old bedroom at my parents' house. I'm just going to say this, long distance does not agree with me. Or rather, it does not agree with the overthinking introvert that is me. Noticing how I changed during our time apart makes me uncomfortable. I became jealous, recreating images and scenarios of what Andrew is doing (in places I had not even Googled – the true strength of my imagination revealed) and overanalysing any mention of the word 'we'. This is not who I am. The obsessive overthinker, yes, fine, that part of me exists (and should be kept in check), but I am not the wife who doubts or distrusts her husband. Not for a second. The fear of the unknown stretched my imagination's skills and sharpened my obsessive compulsions more than I care to admit... Yet here I am admitting it anyway for the sake of this book and comforting others who may experience the same obsessive overwhelm.

On the night of my second moment, Andrew went out for dinner with colleagues who had also recently arrived in the country. The environment wasn't something he expected to experience in a conservative country - a restaurant turned party vibe. My interpretation of his description, from 12 000 km away, imagined women with loose inhibitions everywhere (so dramatic, I know). All

I knew for certain was that I was not there. And not like, 'Aw, I'm missing out!' but, 'What. Is. Really. Happening?'. I tried to calm myself down, it was ten p.m., and I was headed towards a panic attack, so I messaged him goodnight to try and sleep it off. About fifteen minutes later I was rapid-fire messaging him to find out what was going on, why they had not left yet; then when they left, why he was not going back to his flat; and then wanting to know who was still there and, and, and…

I broke. I lost my filter (and all sense of logic) and fixated on the assumptions I made about the evening. I know I said hurtful things, and I know I was looking to hurt because I felt I needed him to know what I was feeling. It took too long for me to realise I was only feeling hurt because I chose to recall my association of a night out that ended with my ex cheating with his 'just a friend' and imposing it on Andrew on his first night out with new friends.

One night a couple of years ago, I could tell by text that my ex had had too much to drink, I knew he was out with a female friend and that they weren't heading home when he said they would be. It didn't end well for me. That night I cried myself to sleep in the same bed I would find myself having a panic attack about my husband years later. So, on the night my husband went out to dinner, had a few drinks with a group of friends who all stayed at their table while the restaurant got loud, and later left to continue conversation at one of the couples' apartment where they hung out until one a.m. - nothing suspicious, nothing dishonest, nothing uncomfortable, nothing we haven't done together - I just couldn't. I freaked out. I hurt Andrew and was introduced to parts of myself I didn't recognise nor ever want to be reacquainted with. While I was hurting and accusing Andrew, I was soundlessly heaving, hyperventilating, crying, and throbbing my heart in my old bedroom with a house full of family. My mind noticed the slight similarities and reattached itself to the hurt of the past, and my body followed, pretty accurately despite the years that had passed.

Not once that night did Andrew get upset with me. Not once did he threaten or become defensive. All he did, while I self-destructed and sabotaged our relationship, was love me. Reassured me. Patiently answered my questions. Allowed me to throw accusations. He promised me everything was okay, that there was nothing for me to worry about and that he wished there was more he could do to help. Keep in mind he was with his friends throughout all of this, but still took the time to fuss over me. And when I was done, he loved me some more. Reassured me some more. And, I don't know how, but he calmed me down. He soothed the scar that was burning.

I said goodnight (for real this time) and then I prayed. I held myself, snot and salty tears dried all over my face and pillow, and I thanked God for Andrew. Then I asked for peace. Peace over the hurt in my heart because I do trust my husband, I have full faith in our marriage, and I knew this pain wasn't because of him; and peace over my mind because I know how powerful it can be and how quick it can turn on me if I allow my obsessive, overthinking nature to even flutter to the surface.

The next morning, I felt two things, peace and embarrassment. I was grateful the peace that put me to sleep stayed, but the embarrassment overwhelmed me, and I immediately apologised to Andrew with a now clear mind and heart. We spoke through it a little, he was happy to leave it in the past as it was over, but I needed him to know that I had not been myself; I was hurt and acknowledged that my obsessive mind created it. It's only today, when I started writing this chapter, that I made the connections to my past. That was the physical reaction, hurt and stress I was feeling. In retrospect it's easy to see how my mind threw sensibility out the window and constructed a false scenario; using emotional ties to make it feel so much like reality. But in the moment the only thing I felt was dread that everything I was thinking was the truth and losing that control over my thoughts was terrifying.

We all process trauma our own way. But introverts like me, process trauma, emotional baggage and most other things almost entirely alone and in our minds. We don't want the world to know something is wrong because they might think less of us for it. We don't feel the need to share it with anyone because we've already thought out all possible avenues of advice and passing comments. I know how difficult it can be, so I urge you to find someone who you can talk to. There are people in your life who will comfort and support you through anything, more than you realise.

We think we know ourselves best, yet our obsessive overthinking can blind us into being someone we don't even recognise. Acknowledge the power of your mind and accept that you need to speak it out (or write it out). Verbalising what is running laps around your mind really helps to find a calm and new perspective to understand what may be triggering you, or what exactly you're feeling. You don't need the listener to understand, just getting it out of your brain can be such a release and relief. I am blessed to have a few people with whom I can be confidently vulnerable.

Fellow introverts, try to notice your obsessive thinking, especially over non-existent things, then redirect that association by thinking of at least one positive association. Something you can evoke and grab onto in times of stress or overwhelm. Practice gratitude, prayer, or meditation - distract your mind from the rabbit hole long enough to allow yourself to process your current experiences logically rather than emotionally. If the threat to break continues, find someone to talk to, or write yourself a message and read it from an objective perspective (you know you can be objective because you do it in your mind with others all the time).

To the non-introverts, have patience. The more you react with loud and strong words or don't react at all, the more we obsess over what that means on top of our current stress. Be there, listen, comfort and, most importantly, love. If we are about to break, or have already, let us get it out and try not take it too personally; but also, introverts, be prepared to manage the aftermath of any episode. Every person will react differently, as they are allowed to, and there is no excuse for being unnecessarily mean. You can trust that we will overanalyse everything we have said and thought in the hours to come and will then be open and able to have a true, constructive conversation.

Getting Over It

Sophrosyne

A healthy state of mind, characterized by self-control, moderation, and a deep awareness of one's true self, and resulting in true happiness.

Well, should we have to get over it? Is it necessary to despise, reject and drill introversion out of ourselves? Personal opinion: Uhm, no! Also, how is one supposed to overcome being an introvert in the first place?

There are millions of successfully functioning introverts in the world; many of whom are unsuspecting. Take Emma Watson and Meryl Streep; great examples of people who, because of their fame and open participation in media, events, and organisations, are assumed to be extroverts, but are actually introverts (according to Google).

No one can tell you you're wrong to classify yourself as an introvert or extrovert. There is no one out there better qualified to clarify your personality identification than yourself. You are the one person you're unapologetically (sometimes harshly) honest with, who, through the pilgrimage of self-discovery, knows the truest and falsest aspects of your persona, and who can acknowledge your secrets and appreciate your simplest truths. To be 100 per cent honest with yourself and remain true to that self is sometimes easier said than done. But it's relatively simple to know what you do and don't like. Knowing which situations make you extremely uncomfortable or overwhelmed, and which interactions require more energy than others. Listening to yourself is the easier task, following through with what you need to do can be more difficult, but not impossible.

For whatever reason, introversion seems to have negative connotations surrounding it. As if it's mentally or emotionally 'not okay' to be an introvert. While I acknowledge unhealthy aspects related to some of my introverted traits, it's not something I feel I should dispel from my being or that I should adopt extroversion as a solution. Rather, it's something I should learn to understand and manage so it doesn't control or overwhelm me; something everyone could do regarding their more 'toxic' traits.

I don't need to be told by people who notice my shyness that I need to 'step out of my comfort zone', at least not as often as I am being told. I *know* there is growth in the uncomfortable and how it can be difficult to discover all aspects of yourself when safe in your comfort zone. I do take steps outside of comfort when I know I need to be challenged for new results, regardless of how small. It's just important for me to feel I have the mental and emotional capacity to do so and that I am doing it out of my own volition. As soon as I am told to 'step out' my instinct is to retreat because, in my mind, that means it's becoming something someone else wants to control, which makes me uncomfortable – especially if they don't fully understand the way I operate. Also, of course I'm going to do the exact opposite of what I'm being told, that's basic human nature* (*see: stubbornness).

I know what experiences and realisations are possible from within my safe zone by merely dipping my toes into the unknown waters, and sometimes that is enough for me. Yes, I may be holding on tightly to the railing for fear of being pulled under said water, but progress is progress – don't judge me. It may not sound like a productive space to many, but if I respect it and work with it, I can feel brave enough to step out and possibly fail - finding productivity in the process. Like I said, I know when it's time to be uncomfortable and I listen for that calling to step into growth, albeit selectively. There is immense value that comes from being an introvert and the skills that we are equipped with when we choose to observe, consider, analyse, and map out the path that leads to the bigger picture. I don't see an issue with prepared venturing into a thoroughly-considered unknown – a steady exploration of what is outside of my comfort zone is still operating outside of my comfort zone, it shouldn't matter how I choose to go about it.

There are other advantages to being an introvert, as many as (if not more than – bias opinion) being an extrovert. Our minds operate with intricate detail, empathy makes us incredibly respectful and kind, our intimate connection with our emotions help identify our passions, we are deeply understanding, and our slightly extroverted tendencies bring all those advantages to the fore for all to enjoy. No one has to 'get over' being an introvert. Introverts, don't think you are fundamentally flawed for being an introvert. Everyone else, don't impose or reinforce a societal association of extroverted value onto introverts; please and thank you.

I know there are struggles that come with introversion, but there are ways to manage and turn them into strengths or healthier habits – much like any personality 'flaw'. But to do this, we need to take it at our pace and listen to what our mind tells us. This is how we learn what triggers our anxieties and joys, and how to dissect and understand what we feel. Allow yourself the space to take the responsibility to learn about and from all of your own intricacies. Hopefully, you will learn to love your introversion and, more importantly, yourself in the process. It comes down to learning to manage and use your introverted traits to your advantage. Find the strengths and develop the weaknesses so that, eventually, they won't have the power to overwhelm you as easily. There is always an opportunity to 'grow through what you go through', and understanding your identity and how you think is one of those opportunities.

As much as I am writing this book for others to understand me, my behaviours and how I think; I am forever learning about myself too. Putting my mind's processes to paper has forced me to better understand them which, in turn, has allowed me to write about them. I can appreciate (now) how important and unique this opportunity is. Understanding my mind and accepting my quirks brings logic and rationality to my thinking and dealings with situations - it helps me manage my anxiety and prioritise honest communication.

I understand now that I am never going to please everyone, no matter how many ways I may bend over backwards for them. And that's okay. Frankly, it's a great thing for me. Learning to say no and remain true to myself instead of becoming involved in something where resentment may arise in that relationship, is the mutually beneficial outcome. Learning to rely on those who may not fully understand me but love me regardless and are there for me in the ways I need is another invaluable take-away.

As much as I will always try to help friends and family understand me better – mostly because I don't want to unintentionally hurt their feelings during moments when I may step away or shut down for self-preservation – I will equally try to not take their misunderstandings of my miscommunications personally as that only leads to repetitive loops and unproductive silence.

No matter who you are, acknowledging when you're in the wrong doesn't feel great, more so when you're a highly sensitive introvert who overthinks every little thing until it becomes the biggest thing. There's a culture of defensiveness that has seemed to become the norm in this regard. I'm guilty of it. Whether my intention is based on me being disappointed with myself for being wrong or feeling embarrassed to the point I feel that I need to justify my actions for some reason – wrong is wrong. And owning that is important, especially when it involves another person. Introverts know how to communicate well in every aspect save for perhaps the actual speaking of words. It is difficult, yes, but owning up without beating yourself up is possible. When you learn to tap into your empathy and the peacemaker side of the people-pleaser, it's easy to see how far an apology can go to keep a line of communication open.

There is so much I still have to learn about my introversion and how it affects and improves daily life. So again, no, I don't think you need to or have to get over being an introvert. I don't even think it's a conversation people should be having amongst themselves. How often do you hear about people telling extroverts to be more introverted? Hardly, if at all. Let us introverts be – so long as we're not a harm to ourselves or others. Allow us the opportunity to accept ourselves without pointing out flaws that we consider a personal strength. Learn to understand rather than to impose 'socially correct' behaviours, and we will learn to find our functional way in this world. There is room to grow in introversion as there is for any personality and human being. Circumstances change, and through that change blooms growth and grace to embrace yourself in the newness. The years of life we are blessed with should be filled with more acceptance, open communication, and love for the people we are and the unique joy only we can bring to this world.

I once described myself as 'soft' while listing positive traits. Being an introvert who feels deeply, considers others' emotional states, observes, carefully crafts responses, understands overwhelm, and relies on socks to give me confidence… to me that is strength through the softest, purest parts of who I am. We are all beautiful in our own way and, as long as we aren't harming ourselves or others in the process, it doesn't need to be more complex than that.

We should be proud.

We go through it all,

with scars that show

what we have built

out of what we have.

No one gets it right.

Humans are inherently flawed,

and yet we are able to love,

able to accept and change,

if only we let ourselves.

Strive to live in the light

of all that makes you,

you.

Watch how that shine

can spread as healing

for all.

Think With Me Today

Metanoia

The journey of changing one's mind, heart, self or way of life.

Consider this a letter from the author, an epilogue and acknowledgements of sorts. I found myself struggling with how to incorporate certain events that have occurred in my life since I started the book. I started at 25 and, well, I am now 29 at the time of publishing – exactly 29 if all has gone according to plan and I have managed to publish on my birthday – hip-hip hooray! Let me clarify that nothing written in this book is made up – other than the figments of my overactive imagination and the lovely mind games it played with me and my relationships. It may be further in the past now, but the experiences remain true, and the emotions associated are as true and real as I could portray in my writing.

Most of what has happened between now and when I started writing was the Coronavirus pandemic, moving to a new country and navigating the new landscape that came with all those experiences.

Life has brought many firsts and curve balls since moving to Qatar, but I thought you should know it's been two years, I'm still alive, no I have not been for a wax, Koda has been adopted by a lovely couple and is happy and healthy (without us, the nerve). I have made friends, I go to malls alone, sit poolside on my own (after a year of overthinking and building up to it), and I have been adopted by a beautiful extrovert who goes to church with me, trains me in the gym (she's helped me so much with gym-related anxiety) and lets me look after her two fluffy dogs. Were some of my anxieties warranted? Yes. But they have been manageable, more so than I ever expected.

As I mentioned, adapting to a new space can be easier for introverts because we're not so focussed on meeting new people, but rather on establishing a routine that lets us leave the house at least twice a week. Nevertheless, it is still a challenge to forcibly operate from outside of your comfort zone, possibly without most of our regular comforts. I promise, it does become better. You will find new ways to manage old habits and develop new skills that seemed otherwise unattainable to your introverted self.

I have been through some emotionally and mentally difficult times here but have also (incredibly) found a refreshment of my faith and relationship with God. As surprising as it has been to find God in a country where He is not predominantly worshipped or accepted, it has been so special and evident. I have never experienced such peace and literal joy amidst tribulation until now. And I can testify that this gift of peace God has blessed over my life has changed how the overwhelming aspects of introversion affect my day-to-day. I still have moments of being overwhelmed and of obsessive thinking, but they feel less intense, thanks to Him. And therapy. Therapy has also been amazing.

I started seeing a therapist regarding a specific issue I was experiencing but, naturally, it's a nurturing environment to discover more about oneself and learn how to manage certain traits productively and healthily. Let me tell you, BrainWorking Recursive Therapy® is a life-changer. I have noticed obsessive thoughts literally stop in their tracks before the spiral can develop. I'm not recommending therapy just for introverts or highly sensitive people, but everybody. Everybody can benefit from therapy. Therapy is great.

After the few months it took me to write and edit my first draft, I moved overseas, and my book was left on the backburner. I allowed myself a settling-in period, which turned into a settlement mindset of 'I've technically written the book, nothing more has to come from it. I'm too busy living a not-at-all-busy life in Qatar'. This is where life-coaching helped me focus on resuming work on my book and reigniting the passion that motivated me to write it. With my life-coach's help (my mother), I slowly started putting together my second draft. And in a few months, I had finished my second draft (as I'm writing this, my second draft is complete – this chapter doesn't count, it's new) and I had established a plan of action with support from a second life-coach. Therapy and life-coaching are so valuable – get on it! And while you're working on yourself, send up a prayer of thanks, help, comfort, grace or strength – whatever it is you need.

On that note, a quick but full-of-love-and-appreciation-thank-you to my husband, my family and in-laws who have been incredibly supportive and encouraging from inception to actualisation. It was a frustrating process for the longest time, so thank you all for never giving up on me and my dream for this book. Mother, you know how much you helped to literally get *Think With Me* complete and I am so grateful to you for that. To every friend I mentioned the book to, thank you for holding me accountable and checking up on my progress. Thank you to my reviewers: Dad, Diane, Ilse, Kyra, Lindsey, and Katia (who also designed and created the beautiful cover) and my editor, Astri; all your insights were exactly what I needed to focus and finish this book. I appreciate the value each of you provided. I could go into detail thanking each individual person, including everyone who ever shared their life experiences with me, which added to my mental library of empathy and understanding... but that could be another book; you know who you are and your contribution. God, thank you for making me *me;* with my gifts, talents, personality and all the incredible people You have blessed my life with; the sense of purpose I experienced writing this book could only have come from You.

This book has been a journey in the most needed way. I am so excited and anxious (happy anxious) for what is to come. I hope you have enjoyed my story; I really did enjoy writing it. Now, go tell your people you love them, reach out when you need to (and there will always be a time of need), love the uniqueness of your personality and continuously attempt to grow through every situation.

To those I know, and to those I don't know (yet), I love you.

The end.

Fin.

Time to move onto the next to-be-read book on your list.

Okay, bye!

Notes

1. Grimes, J.M., Cheek, J.M., Grimes, J., and Norem, J. 2011. Four Meanings of Introversion: Social, Thinking, Anxious, and Inhibited Introversion.

P.S. From the Author

I want to say a quick thank you for supporting me by reading this book. I truly hope you found value in what I shared and know that your support means so much to this first-time self-published author. Please leave a review on Amazon, Takealot, Goodreads or wherever you stumbled across *Think With Me*. You can also directly message me on Instagram @thelowe.lywriter, I would love to chat with you! And if you follow The Lowe-ly Writer you can stay updated on any new projects and see a few of my other writing pieces.

Love,

Tasmin

www.ingramcontent.com/pod-product-compliance
Lightning Source LLC
Chambersburg PA
CBHW070114070426
42448CB00039B/2792